THE ANTI-ANXIETY DIET COOKBOOK

DISCOVER OVER 75 DELICIOUS, EASY-TO-PREPARE RECIPES DESIGNED TO NOURISH YOUR BODY, SUPPORT MENTAL WELLNESS, AND PROMOTE A SENSE OF CALM.

KRISTINA J. ALBINO

TABLE OF CONTENT

INTRODUCTION

In today's fast-paced world, finding tranquility and maintaining mental wellness can often feel like an uphill battle. We're constantly juggling responsibilities, facing unexpected challenges, and navigating the complexities of modern life. Stress and anxiety can take a toll on our well-being, but what if there was a way to ease these burdens through something as fundamental as the food we eat? Welcome to The Anti-Anxiety Diet Cookbook: A Comprehensive Guide to Stress-Relief Through Food, Featuring Delicious and Easy-to-Prepare Meals to Support Mental Wellness and Overall Health.

Why Food Matters for Mental Wellness

Our diet plays a crucial role in how we feel. Nutrient-rich foods can enhance mood, stabilize energy levels, and support overall mental health. By focusing on foods that help manage stress and promote relaxation, we can create a powerful foundation for well-being. This cookbook is designed to guide you through that journey, offering 100 carefully crafted recipes that are not only delicious but also tailored to support your mental wellness.

A Holistic Approach to Stress-Relief

This cookbook goes beyond simply providing recipes. It introduces you to the principles of mindful eating and holistic nutrition, emphasizing how certain ingredients can positively impact your mental state. Each recipe is crafted with ingredients known for their calming and stress-relieving properties, helping to create a balanced diet that supports emotional resilience and mental clarity.

Easy-to-Prepare Meals for Everyday Living

We understand that life is busy, and that's why this cookbook features easy-to-prepare meals that fit seamlessly into your daily routine. Whether you're a novice cook or a seasoned chef, you'll find recipes that are simple, quick, and satisfying. From hearty breakfasts to comforting dinners and soothing snacks, each dish is designed to nourish both your body and your mind.

Nutritious Breakfasts:

Start your day on a positive note with meals that set the tone for a calm and balanced day ahead. Discover recipes like the calming chia seed pudding and energizing green smoothie to kick start your morning.

Relaxing Lunches:

Enjoy midday meals that help maintain steady energy levels and a clear mind. Options such as the serene spinach and feta stuffed chicken or the gentle quinoa salad offer both nutrition and tranquility.

Comforting Dinners:

End your day with soothing dishes that promote relaxation and support a restful night's sleep. Try recipes like the tranquil turmeric rice or the mellow mushroom risotto for a comforting end to your day.

Mindful Snacks:

Discover snacks that provide a moment of calm during hectic days. From blissful blueberry banana bread to calming mint chocolate bites, these snacks are perfect for a quick stress-relief boost.

Calming Beverages:

Sip on drinks designed to reduce stress and enhance overall well-being. Enjoy calming turmeric tea or a serene herbal green juice for a soothing drink that complements your meals.

Stress-Relief Strategies:

Learn about the key nutrients and ingredients known for their stress-relieving properties. Each section includes tips on how to incorporate these into your diet for maximum benefit.

Mindful Eating Practices:

Explore techniques for mindful eating that can help you enjoy your food more fully and reduce stress. Discover how paying attention to your meals can enhance your overall well-being.

Meal Planning and Preparation Tips:

Find practical advice on how to plan and prepare meals ahead of time to make your life easier and reduce stress. Learn how to create a meal plan that supports your mental wellness goals.

Understanding Stress-Relief Ingredients:

Dive into a detailed guide on ingredients that are known to combat anxiety and stress. Learn about the benefits of turmeric, omega-3s, magnesium, and more, and how to effectively incorporate them into your diet.

Creating a Relaxing Dining Environment:

Discover tips for setting up a calming dining space that enhances you're eating experience. Simple changes in your environment can make mealtime more relaxing and enjoyable.

Personalized Meal Plans:

Explore sample meal plans tailored to different stress levels and dietary needs. Find out how to customize your meals to best suit your lifestyle and wellness goals.

Boosting Your Mood with Spices and Herbs:

Learn about specific spices and herbs known for their mood-enhancing properties. Recipes featuring ingredients like saffron, chamomile, and valerian root offer natural ways to boost your mood and reduce anxiety.

Incorporating Mindfulness into Meal Prep:

Explore methods to bring mindfulness into your meal preparation process. From cooking techniques that enhance relaxation to mindful eating practices, discover how to turn cooking into a calming ritual.

Balancing Macronutrients for Mental Clarity:

Understand how balancing proteins, fats, and carbohydrates can affect mental clarity and stress levels. Recipes are designed to help you achieve a balanced macronutrient profile that supports cognitive function and emotional balance.

The Role of Hydration in Stress Management:

Discover the importance of staying hydrated and its impact on stress levels. Learn about hydrating recipes and beverages that keep you refreshed and support mental wellness.

BENEFITS OF THIS COOKBOOK

Enhanced Mental Wellness:

Each recipe is designed with ingredients that promote relaxation, reduce anxiety, and support overall mental health.

Improved Mood:

Enjoy meals that help stabilize mood swings and enhance emotional resilience.

Reduced Stress:

The cookbook provides recipes that include stress-relief nutrients and calming ingredients to help manage daily stress.

Better Sleep:

Discover dishes that support restful sleep, helping you wake up refreshed and ready to face the day.

Convenient and Easy:

Recipes are simple to prepare, fitting into even the busiest of schedules without compromising on quality or taste.

Holistic Health:

Gain a deeper understanding of how diet impacts mental wellness and learn how to integrate stress-relief strategies into your everyday meals.

CAN YOU EAT AND CAN'T EAT?

Can Eat:
Whole Grains:

Oats, quinoa, brown rice, and barley support stable blood sugar levels and provide essential nutrients.

Lean Proteins:

Chicken, turkey, tofu, and fish offer the amino acids necessary for mood regulation.

Healthy Fats:

Avocados, nuts, seeds, and olive oil contribute to brain health and stress reduction.

Fruits and Vegetables: Berries, leafy greens, bananas, and sweet potatoes are rich in antioxidants and vitamins that support mental wellness.

Herbs and Spices:

Turmeric, ginger, chamomile, and lavender are known for their calming properties and can be incorporated into various dishes.

Processed Foods:

Foods high in refined sugars and artificial additives can negatively impact mood and increase stress.

Caffeine:

Excessive caffeine can exacerbate anxiety and disrupt sleep patterns.

Excessive Alcohol:

Alcohol can interfere with mental health and contribute to increased anxiety and stress.

High-Sodium Foods: Foods with high sodium content can contribute to high blood pressure and exacerbate stress.

Stock Your Pantry:

Keep a well-stocked pantry with stress-relief staples like turmeric, chia seeds, and dark leafy greens to make meal preparation easier.

Meal Prep:

Plan and prep your meals in advance to reduce stress during busy weeks. Prepare ingredients in bulk and store them in portioned containers.

Mindful Eating:

Take time to eat mindfully by focusing on your food and enjoying each bite. This practice helps with digestion and reduces stress.

Experiment with Herbs and Spices:

Try incorporating calming herbs like chamomile or soothing spices like ginger into your recipes for added stress-relief benefits.

Stay Hydrated:

Don't forget the importance of hydration. Include recipes for hydrating beverages to maintain optimal mental and physical health.

Comprehensive Guidance:

This cookbook offers a complete guide to using food as a tool for managing anxiety and stress.

Variety of Recipes:

With 100 diverse recipes, you'll find plenty of options to keep your meals interesting and enjoyable.

Personalized Solutions:

Recipes and meal plans are tailored to different stress levels and dietary needs, providing solutions that fit your unique lifestyle.

Educational Insight:

Gain knowledge about stress-relief ingredients and holistic nutrition, empowering you to make informed dietary choices.

Enhanced Well-Being:

Embrace a holistic approach to mental wellness, combining nutritious food with mindful eating practices to foster a balanced and serene life.

YOUR JOURNEY TO WELLNESS BEGINS HERE

With The Anti-Anxiety Diet Cookbook, you're not just adding new recipes to your repertoire; you're embarking on a journey towards a more peaceful, balanced, and healthy lifestyle. Embrace the power of food to transform your mental wellness and find comfort in every meal. Let's cook, nourish, and thrive together.

Exploring the Cookbook

As you delve into this cookbook, remember that each recipe is more than just a dish; it's a step towards a more serene and balanced life. Whether you're looking to manage daily stress or seeking a more mindful way of eating, this book provides the tools you need to support your mental health through nourishing food.

Enjoy exploring these recipes and discovering the soothing benefits of mindful eating. Here's to a more serene and healthful life through the power of delicious, stress-relief-focused meals.

-----------------RECIPES-----------------

1. CALM AND COZY OATMEAL BOWL

Servings: 2 | Prep Time: 5 min | Cook Time: 10 min

INGREDIENTS:

- ❖ 1 cups of rolled oats
- ❖ 2 cups of almond milk
- ❖ 1 tbsp chia seeds
- ❖ 1 tsp cinnamon
- ❖ 1 tbsp honey or maple syrup
- ❖ 1/2 tsp vanilla extract
- ❖ 1/4 cups of blueberries
- ❖ 1/4 cup of chop-up walnuts
- ❖ 1 tbsp flax seeds

INSTRUCTIONS:

1. Mix the almond milk & oats in a medium saucepan and boil.
2. Stir in vanilla essence, cinnamon, and chia seeds. Mix thoroughly.
3. Cook, stirring periodically, until the oats are soft and creamy, 7 to 10 min.
4. Take off the heat and mix in the maple syrup or honey.
5. Spoon the porridge into two separate dishes. Add flax seeds, walnuts, and blueberries on top.
6. Warm-up and savor your comforting, peaceful oatmeal.

NUTRITION INFO:

Calories: 350 | Protein: 10g | Carbs: 55g | Fat: 12g | Fiber: 9g | Sugar: 12g

2. SERENITY SMOOTHIE

Servings: 1 | Prep Time: 5 min | Cook Time: 0 min

INGREDIENTS:

- 1 banana
- 1/2 cup of spinach leaves
- 1/2 avocado
- 1/2 cup of unsweetened almond milk
- 1 tbsp almond butter
- 1 tbsp chia seeds
- 1/2 tsp vanilla extract
- 1/2 cup of ice cubes

INSTRUCTIONS:

1. In a blender, add the banana, spinach, avocado, chia seeds, almond butter, almond milk, vanilla essence, and ice cubes.
2. Blend till creamy and smooth.
3. Transfer to a glass and enjoy your calm, revitalizing smoothie.

NUTRITION INFO:

Calories: 300 | Protein: 5g | Carbs: 40g | Fat: 15g | Fiber: 10g | Sugar: 15g

3. TRANQUIL TURMERIC LATTE

Servings: 1 | Prep Time: 5 min | Cook Time: 5 min

INGREDIENTS:

- 1 cup of unsweetened almond milk
- 1/2 tsp ground turmeric
- 1/4 tsp ground cinnamon
- 1/4 tsp ground ginger
- 1/2 tsp vanilla extract
- 1 tsp honey or maple syrup
- Pinch of black pepper

INSTRUCTIONS:

1. Warm, but not boiling, almond milk should be heated in a tiny saucepan over medium heat.
2. Add the black pepper, vanilla essence, cinnamon, ginger, turmeric, and honey or maple syrup and whisk.
3. Keep whisking until the latte is foamy and all the ingredients are thoroughly blended.
4. Pour into a cup of, then enjoy your soothing, warm turmeric latte.

NUTRITION INFO:

Calories: 80 | Protein: 1g | Carbs: 12g | Fat: 3g | Fiber: 1g | Sugar: 9g

4. PEACEFUL PESTO PASTA

Servings: 4 | Prep Time: 10 min | Cook Time: 15 min

INGREDIENTS:

- 8 oz whole wheat pasta
- 2 cups of fresh basil leaves
- 1/4 cup of pine nuts
- 2 cloves garlic
- 1/4 cups finely grated Parmesan cheese
- 1/3 cup of extra-virgin olive oil
- 1/2 tsp salt
- 1/4 tsp black pepper
- 1/4 cup of cherry tomatoes, halved (non-compulsory)

INSTRUCTIONS:

1. When cooking pasta, be sure to follow the package guidelines. After draining, put it away.
2. Basil leaves, pine nuts, garlic, Parmesan cheese, pepper, & salt should all be mixd in a food processor. Pulse until chop-up lightly.
3. Once the machine is operating, gradually add the olive oil and process until the pesto becomes creamy and silky.
4. Coat the cooked pasta evenly with the pesto by tossing it in it.
5. Serve warm, with cherry tomatoes on top if desired.

NUTRITION INFO:

Calories: 360 | Protein: 10g | Carbs: 45g | Fat: 17g | Fiber: 6g | Sugar: 2g

5. RELAXING RASPBERRY CHIA PUDDING

Servings: 2 | Prep Time: 5 min | Cook Time: 4 hrs (chill time)

INGREDIENTS:

- 1 cup of unsweetened almond milk
- 1/4 cups of chia seeds
- 1 tbsp maple syrup or honey
- 1/2 tsp vanilla extract
- 1/2 cups of fresh raspberries
- 1 tbsp shredded coconut (non-compulsory)

INSTRUCTIONS:

1. Mix almond milk, chia seeds, maple syrup, and vanilla essence in a container or dish.
2. To avoid clumping, cover, and chill for at least 4 hrs or overnight, stirring now and again.
3. Stir the chia pudding and divide it between two bowls when you're ready to serve.
4. If preferred, garnish with shredded coconut and fresh raspberries.
5. Savor the tranquility of your raspberry chia pudding.

NUTRITION INFO:

Calories: 200 | Protein: 5g | Carbs: 25g | Fat: 10g | Fiber: 12g | Sugar: 10g

6. COMFORTING QUINOA SALAD

Servings: 4 | Prep Time: 10 min | Cook Time: 15 min

INGREDIENTS:

- 1 cup of quinoa, rinsed
- 2 cups of water
- 1 cup of cherry tomatoes, halved
- 1 cucumber, diced
- 1/4 cup of red onion, lightly chop-up
- 1/4 cup of feta cheese, crumbled
- 2 tbsp fresh parsley, chop-up
- 1/4 cup of extra-virgin olive oil
- 2 tbsp lemon juice
- 1/2 tsp salt
- 1/4 tsp black pepper

INSTRUCTIONS:

1. Bring water and quinoa to a boil in a medium-sized pot. For fifteen min, or until the water is absorbed and the quinoa is fluffy, reduce heat, cover, and simmer. Allow it to cool a little.
2. The cooked quinoa, cherry tomatoes, cucumber, red onion, feta cheese, and parsley should all be mixd in a big bowl.
3. Mix the lemon juice, olive oil, pepper, & salt in a small bowl. Dollop onto the quinoa salad and mix to ensure uniform coating.
4. Serve either room temp. Or cold. Savor the warmth of your quinoa salad.

NUTRITION INFO:

Calories: 250 | Protein: 7g | Carbs: 30g | Fat: 12g | Fiber: 4g | Sugar: 3g

7. SOOTHING SWEET POTATO SOUP

Servings: 4 | Prep Time: 10 min | Cook Time: 30 min

INGREDIENTS:

- 2 large sweet potatoes, peeled and cubed
- 1 onion, chop-up
- 2 cloves garlic, chop-up
- 4 cups of vegetable broth
- 1 tsp ground cumin
- 1/2 tsp ground cinnamon
- 1/2 tsp ground ginger
- 1/4 tsp cayenne pepper (non-compulsory)
- 1/2 cups of coconut milk
- Pepper, & salt as needed

INSTRUCTIONS:

1. Add the onion and garlic to a large saucepan and sauté over medium heat until softened, approximately 5 min.
2. Add the cayenne pepper (if using), cumin, cinnamon, ginger, and sweet potatoes to the vegetable broth. Once they have reached a boil, lower the heat & cook the sweet potatoes until they are soft, for about 20 min.
3. The soup may be pureed to a creamy consistency using an immersion blender. Add the coconut milk and taste-test to adjust the seasoning.
4. Enjoy your comforting sweet potato soup while it's still warm.

NUTRITION INFO:

Calories: 180 | Protein: 3g | Carbs: 32g | Fat: 6g | Fiber: 6g | Sugar: 7g

8. GENTLE GREEN DETOX JUICE

Servings: 1 | Prep Time: 5 min | Cook Time: 0 min

INGREDIENTS:

- 1 cucumber, chop-up
- 2 celery stalks, chop-up
- 1 green apple, cored and chop-up
- 1 cup of spinach leaves
- 1/2 lemon, juiced
- 1-inch piece of ginger, peeled
- 1/2 cups of water

INSTRUCTIONS:

1. Pulse everything together until it's completely smooth in a blender.
2. If you would want the juice to have a smoother consistency, strain it through cheesecloth or a fine mesh screen.
3. Pour into a glass and enjoy your somewhat detoxifying green drink.

NUTRITION INFO:

Calories: 90 | Protein: 2g | Carbs: 20g | Fat: 0.5g | Fiber: 5g | Sugar: 10g

9. BLISSFUL BLUEBERRY MUFFINS

Servings: 12 muffins | Prep Time: 10 min | Cook Time: 20 min

INGREDIENTS:

- 2 cup whole wheat flour
- 1/2 cup rolled oats
- 1/2 cups of honey or maple syrup
- 1 tsp baking powder
- 1/2 tsp baking soda
- 1/2 tsp salt
- 1 tsp cinnamon
- 1 cup of unsweetened almond milk
- 1/4 cup of coconut oil, melted
- 2 large eggs
- 1 tsp vanilla extract
- 1 1/2 cup fresh / frozen blueberries

INSTRUCTIONS:

1. As you prepare a muffin tray, line it with paper liners and preheat your oven temp. to 350°F/175°C.
2. Mix the flour, oats, baking soda, baking powder, salt, and cinnamon together in a big basin.
3. Mix the eggs, honey or maple syrup, coconut oil, almond milk, & vanilla extract in a separate bowl.
4. Mixing until just mixed, pour the wet components into the dry ingredients. Fold in the blueberries gently.
5. Spoon the batter into each muffin pan.
6. After 20 to 25 min in the oven, remove the toothpick.
7. Allow to cool for five min, then move to a wire rack. Savor the joyous blueberry muffins.

NUTRITION INFO:

Calories: 160 | Protein: 4g | Carbs: 25g | Fat: 5g | Fiber: 3g | Sugar: 10g

10. HARMONY HERBAL TEA BLEND

Servings: 4 cups of | Prep Time: 5 min | Cook Time: 10 min

INGREDIENTS:

- 2 tbsp dried chamomile flowers
- 1 tbsp dried lemon balm
- 1 tbsp dried peppermint
- 1 tsp dried lavender
- 1 tsp dried rose petals
- 4 cups of boiling water
- Honey or lemon (non-compulsory)

INSTRUCTIONS:

1. The chamomile, peppermint, lavender, rose petals, and lemon balm should all be mixd in a big cup of or teapot.
2. Cover the herbs with the boiling water and steep for ten min.
3. Pour tea through a strainer into mugs, and if preferred, sweeten with honey or lemon.
4. Enjoy your harmonious herbal tea mix by taking a leisurely sip.

NUTRITION INFO:

Calories: 0 | Protein: 0g | Carbs: 0g | Fat: 0g | Fiber: 0g | Sugar: 0g

11. BALANCED BALSAMIC GLAZED SALMON

Servings: 4 | Prep Time: 10 min | Cook Time: 15 min

INGREDIENTS:

- 4 salmon fillets (about 6 oz every)
- 1/4 cups of balsamic vinegar
- 2 tbsp honey
- 1 tbsp Dijon mustard
- 1 tbsp olive oil
- 2 cloves garlic, chop-up
- Pepper, & salt as needed
- Fresh parsley for garnish

INSTRUCTIONS:

1. Set oven temp. to 400°F, or 200°C.
2. Mix the olive oil, honey, Dijon mustard, balsamic vinegar, and garlic in a small bowl.
3. Arrange the salmon fillets onto a parchment paper-lined baking sheet. Add pepper and salt for seasoning.
4. Drizzle the salmon fillets with the balsamic glaze.
5. Bake the salmon for 12 to 15 min, or until it is cooked through and flake readily when tested with a fork.
6. Serve warm, garnished with fresh parsley. Savor the well-balanced fish with a balsamic glaze.

NUTRITION INFO:

Calories: 320 | Protein: 34g | Carbs: 10g | Fat: 16g | Fiber: 0g | Sugar: 8g

12. STRESS-FREE STIR-FRY

Servings: 4 | Prep Time: 10 min | Cook Time: 15 min

INGREDIENTS:

- 2 tbsp sesame oil
- 1 onion, split
- 2 cloves garlic, chop-up
- 1 bell pepper, split
- 1 carrot, julienned
- 1 zucchini, split
- 1 cup of broccoli florets
- 1/4 cups soy sauce or tamari
- 1 tbsp rice vinegar
- 1 tbsp honey or maple syrup
- 1 tsp finely grated ginger
- 1/4 tsp red pepper flakes (non-compulsory)
- 1/4 cup of chop-up green onions
- Cooked brown rice or noodles, for serving

INSTRUCTIONS:

1. Sesame oil should be heated in a large wok or pan over medium-high heat.
2. Add garlic & onion, and cook for two to three min, or until aromatic.
3. Add the broccoli, zucchini, bell pepper, and carrot. Sauté the veggies for five to seven min, or until they are crisp-tender.
4. Mix the soy sauce, rice vinegar, ginger, honey, and red pepper flakes in a small bowl.
5. After pouring the sauce over the veggies, toss to ensure uniform coating. Simmer for a further two min.
6. Add some green onions as a garnish, & serve over noodles or brown rice. Savor your stir-fry without worrying.

NUTRITION INFO:

Calories: 200 | Protein: 5g | Carbs: 25g | Fat: 10g | Fiber: 4g | Sugar: 8g

13. MINDFUL MATCHA ENERGY BITES

Servings: 12 bites | Prep Time: 10 min | Cook Time: 0 min (chill time: 1 hr)

INGREDIENTS:

- 1 cups of rolled oats
- 1/2 cups of almond butter
- 1/4 cups honey or maple syrup
- 1 tbsp matcha powder
- 1/4 cups of shredded coconut
- 1/4 cups of dark chocolate chips
- 1/2 tsp vanilla extract

INSTRUCTIONS:

1. The rolled oats, almond butter, honey, matcha powder, dark chocolate chips, shredded coconut, and vanilla essence should all be mixd in a big bowl.
2. Mixing the components thoroughly requires stirring.
3. Form the mixture into twelve little balls, then arrange them on a parchment paper-lined baking sheet.
4. To firm up, chill in the refrigerator for a minimum of one hr.
5. Savor your mindful matcha energy bites for a stress-relieving, fast snack.

NUTRITION INFO:

Calories: 120 | Protein: 3g | Carbs: 15g | Fat: 6g | Fiber: 2g | Sugar: 7g

14. CALMING COCONUT CURRY

Servings: 4 | Prep Time: 10 min | Cook Time: 25 min

INGREDIENTS:

- 1 tbsp coconut oil
- 1 onion, chop-up
- 2 cloves garlic, chop-up
- 1 tbsp fresh ginger, finely grated
- 1 tbsp curry powder
- 1 tsp ground turmeric
- 1/2 tsp ground cumin
- 1/4 tsp cayenne pepper (non-compulsory)
- 1 can (14 oz) coconut milk
- 1 can (14 oz) diced tomatoes
- 1 cup of cauliflower florets
- 1 cup of chickpeas, drained and rinsed
- 1 large carrot, split
- 1 cups of spinach leaves
- Pepper, & salt as needed
- Fresh cilantro for garnish
- Cooked brown rice or quinoa, for serving

INSTRUCTIONS:

1. In a large saucepan set over medium heat, warm the coconut oil. Add onion, garlic, & ginger, and cook for approximately 5 min, or until the onion becomes transparent.
2. Add the turmeric, cumin, curry powder, and cayenne pepper (if using), and simmer for one min, or until aromatic.
3. Simmer after adding the chop-up tomatoes and coconut milk.
4. Cook the carrot, cauliflower, and chickpeas for 15 min or until the veggies are soft.
5. Add the spinach and simmer, stirring, until it wilts. As needed, add pepper, & salt for seasoning.
6. Serve over cooked quinoa / brown rice & top with fresh cilantro. Cheers to your soothing curry of coconut.

NUTRITION INFO:

Calories: 320 | Protein: 8g | Carbs: 30g | Fat: 20g | Fiber: 8g | Sugar: 7g

15. ZEN ZUCCHINI NOODLES WITH PESTO

Servings: 2 | Prep Time: 10 min | Cook Time: 5 min

INGREDIENTS:

- 2 medium zucchinis, spiralized
- 1 cup of fresh basil leaves
- 1/4 cup of pine nuts
- 2 cloves garlic
- 1/4 cups Parmesan cheese, finely grated
- 1/4 cup of extra-virgin olive oil
- 1/4 tsp salt
- 1/4 tsp black pepper
- Cherry tomatoes, halved (non-compulsory)

INSTRUCTIONS:

1. Basil leaves, pine nuts, garlic, Parmesan cheese, pepper, & salt should all be mixd in a food processor. Pulse until chop-up lightly.
2. Once the machine is operating, gradually add the olive oil and process until the pesto becomes creamy and silky.
3. The zucchini noodles should be slightly softened after two to three min of medium-high heat cooking in a big pan.
4. Once the zucchini noodles are appropriately coated, toss them with the pesto.
5. Serve warm, with cherry tomatoes on top if desired. Savor your zen pesto-topped zucchini noodles.

NUTRITION INFO:

Calories: 220 | Protein: 6g | Carbs: 10g | Fat: 18g | Fiber: 3g | Sugar: 4g

16. TRANQUIL TAHINI DRESSING

Servings: 4 | Prep Time: 5 min | Cook Time: 0 min

INGREDIENTS:

- 1/4 cups of tahini
- 2 tbsp lemon juice
- 1 tbsp maple syrup or honey
- 1 clove garlic, chop-up
- 2-3 tbsp water (to thin)
- Pepper, & salt as needed

INSTRUCTIONS:

1. Mix the tahini, lemon juice, honey or maple syrup, and garlic in a small bowl.
2. One spoonful at a time, gradually add water until the dressing has the consistency you want.
3. As needed, add pepper, & salt for seasoning.
4. Pour over roasted veggies, grain bowls, and salads. Savor the peace of your tahini dressing.

NUTRITION INFO:

Calories: 100 | Protein: 3g | Carbs: 7g | Fat: 8g | Fiber: 2g | Sugar: 3g

17. PEACEFUL PUMPKIN SOUP

Servings: 4 | Prep Time: 10 min | Cook Time: 20 min

INGREDIENTS:

- 1 tbsp olive oil
- 1 onion, chop-up
- 2 cloves garlic, chop-up
- 1 tsp ground cumin
- 1/2 tsp ground cinnamon
- 1/4 tsp ground nutmeg
- 1 can (15 oz) pumpkin puree
- 3 cups of vegetable broth
- 1/2 cups of coconut milk
- Pepper, & salt as needed
- Pumpkin seeds for garnish (non-compulsory)

INSTRUCTIONS:

1. A large saucepan over medium heat should be used to heat the olive oil. Sauté the onion and garlic for around five min or until they are tender.
2. Add the nutmeg, cinnamon, and cumin and simmer, stirring, for 1 min, until aromatic.
3. Simmer after adding the vegetable broth and pumpkin purée. Cook, stirring periodically, for ten min.
4. Add the coconut milk and taste-test to adjust the seasoning.
5. Smooth up the soup by blending it in stages or using an immersion blender.
6. If preferred, top heated servings with pumpkin seeds. Savor the tranquility of your pumpkin soup.

NUTRITION INFO:

Calories: 150 | Protein: 3g | Carbs: 18g | Fat: 8g | Fiber: 4g | Sugar: 6g

18. MELLOW MUSHROOM RISOTTO

Servings: 4 | Prep Time: 10 min | Cook Time: 30 min

INGREDIENTS:

- 1 tbsp olive oil
- 1 onion, lightly chop-up
- 2 cloves garlic, chop-up
- 1 cup of Arborio rice
- 1/2 cups of white wine (non-compulsory)
- 4 cups of vegetable broth, kept warm
- 2 cups of mushrooms, split (such as cremini or button)
- 1/2 cups finely grated Parmesan cheese
- 2 tbsp fresh parsley, chop-up
- Pepper, & salt as needed

INSTRUCTIONS:

1. Olive oil should be heated in a big skillet over medium heat. Sauté the onion and garlic for around five min or until they are tender.
2. Once the rice is gently browned, stir in the Arborio and simmer for one to two min.
3. Add the white wine, if using, and heat until it is absorbed.
4. One cup at a time, start adding the heated vegetable broth, stirring often and letting the liquid permeate before adding more.
5. The mushrooms should be soft and caramelized after being sautéed over medium heat in a separate pan.
6. Add the mushrooms, Parmesan cheese, and parsley once the risotto is creamy and the rice is soft, which should take 20 to 25 min. As needed, add pepper, & salt for seasoning.
7. Enjoy your velvety mushroom risotto warm out of the pot.

NUTRITION INFO:

Calories: 320 | Protein: 10g | Carbs: 45g | Fat: 12g | Fiber: 3g | Sugar: 4g

19. STRESS-RELIEF STUFFED PEPPERS

Servings: 4 | Prep Time: 15 min | Cook Time: 30 min

INGREDIENTS:

- 4 bell peppers (any color)
- 1 cups of cooked quinoa
- Black beans, 15 ounces (can), washed and drained
- 1 cups of corn kernels (fresh or frozen)
- 1/2 cups of diced tomatoes
- 1/2 cups shredded cheese (cheddar or Monterey Jack)
- 1 tsp cumin
- 1 tsp paprika
- 1/2 tsp garlic powder
- Pepper, & salt as needed
- Fresh cilantro for garnish

INSTRUCTIONS:

1. Set the oven temp. to 375°F, or 190°C.
2. Slice off the bell peppers' tops, then take out the seeds and membranes.
3. Cooked quinoa, black beans, corn, chop-up tomatoes, cheese, cumin, paprika, garlic powder, pepper, & salt should all be mixd in a big bowl.
4. After packing the quinoa mixture into the bell peppers, put them in a baking dish.
5. Bake the peppers for 25 to 30 min, or until they are soft.
6. Before serving, garnish with fresh cilantro. Savor your filled peppers as a stress reliever.

NUTRITION INFO:

Calories: 270 | Protein: 10g | Carbs: 35g | Fat: 10g | Fiber: 8g | Sugar: 6g

20. QUIET QUINOA BUDDHA BOWL

Servings: 2 | Prep Time: 15 min | Cook Time: 15 min

INGREDIENTS:

- 1 cups of cooked quinoa
- 1 cup of roasted chickpeas (see note below)
- 1 cup of cherry tomatoes, halved
- 1 avocado, split
- 1 cups of baby spinach
- 1/4 cups of feta cheese, crumbled
- 2 tbsp tahini dressing (see recipe above)
- 1 tbsp lemon juice
- Pepper, & salt as needed

INSTRUCTIONS:

1. Spoon the cooked quinoa into two separate dishes.
2. Add roasted chickpeas, feta cheese, cherry tomatoes, avocado slices, and baby spinach on top.
3. Pour lemon juice and tahini dressing over it.
4. As needed, add pepper, & salt for seasoning. Savor your peaceful Buddha bowl of quinoa.

NUTRITION INFO:

Calories: 350 | Protein: 12g | Carbs: 45g | Fat: 16g | Fiber: 10g | Sugar: 7g

NOTE: For roasted chickpeas, toss 1 can of chickpeas (drained and rinsed) with 1 tsp of paprika, 1 tbsp of olive oil, & 1/2 tsp of garlic powder. Roast at 400°F (200°C) for 20 min, stirring halfway through.

21. BALANCED BANANA PANCAKES

Servings: 4 (8 pancakes) | Prep Time: 10 min | Cook Time: 15 min

INGREDIENTS:

- 1 cup of whole wheat flour
- 1 tbsp baking powder
- 1/2 tsp salt
- 1 tbsp honey or maple syrup
- 1 large banana, mashed
- 1 cups of unsweetened almond milk
- 1 egg
- 1/2 tsp vanilla extract
- Cooking spray or a small amount of oil for the pan

INSTRUCTIONS:

1. Mix the baking powder, flour, & salt in a large basin.
2. The mashed banana, almond milk, egg, vanilla extract, and honey or maple syrup should all be mixd in a separate bowl.
3. Mixing until just mixed, pour the wet components into the dry ingredients. It's okay if there are some lumps in the batter.
4. Apply a thin layer of cooking spray / oil to a nonstick pan or griddle before heating it up to medium heat.
5. For every pancake, pour 1/4 cups of batter onto the skillet and heat it until bubbles appear on top. After turning, cook the other side until it becomes golden brown.
6. Top with your preferred toppings and serve warm. Savor your nutritious pancakes with bananas.

NUTRITION INFO:

Calories: 220 | Protein: 6g | Carbs: 35g | Fat: 6g | Fiber: 4g | Sugar: 10g

22. HARMONY HERBAL CHICKEN

Servings: 4 | Prep Time: 10 min | Cook Time: 25 min

INGREDIENTS:

- 4 boneless, skinless chicken breasts
- 2 tbsp olive oil
- 1 tsp dried thyme
- 1 tsp dried rosemary
- 1 tsp dried sage
- 2 cloves garlic, chop-up
- 1/2 cups of chicken broth
- 1 lemon, split
- Pepper, & salt as needed

INSTRUCTIONS:

1. Set the oven temp. to 375°F, or 190°C.
2. Olive oil should be used to rub the chicken breasts before adding salt, pepper, thyme, rosemary, and sage.
3. The chicken breasts should be poured into a baking dish together with the chicken stock.
4. Place a couple of slices of lemon on top of every chicken breast.
5. Bake the chicken for 20 to 25 min, or until it is cooked through and 165°F (74°C) inside.
6. Before serving, let it sit for five min. Savor the harmony of your herbal chicken.

NUTRITION INFO:

Calories: 250 | Protein: 35g | Carbs: 1g | Fat: 12g | Fiber: 0g | Sugar: 0g

23. CALM & COLLECTED COUSCOUS

Servings: 4 | Prep Time: 10 min | Cook Time: 10 min

INGREDIENTS:

- 1 cup of couscous
- 1 cups of vegetable broth
- 1 tbsp olive oil
- 1/4 cup of chop-up fresh parsley
- 1/4 cups of chop-up fresh mint
- 1/4 cups of toasted pine nuts
- 1/2 cups of diced cucumber
- 1/2 cup of cherry tomatoes, halved
- 1/4 cups of crumbled feta cheese
- 1 tbsp lemon juice
- Pepper, & salt as needed

INSTRUCTIONS:

1. Heat the vegetable broth in a medium-sized saucepan until it begins to boil. Remove from heat, cover, and stir in the couscous. Please give it a five-min sit.
2. Using a fork, fluff the couscous & then transfer to a large bowl.
3. Add the feta cheese, cucumber, cherry tomatoes, pine nuts, parsley, and mint.
4. Season with pepper, & salt as needed and drizzle with lemon juice.
5. Heat or serve room temp. Savor your peaceful and composed couscous.

NUTRITION INFO:

Calories: 220 | Protein: 7g | Carbs: 30g | Fat: 10g | Fiber: 3g | Sugar: 4g

24. SERENITY SPINACH SALAD

Servings: 4 | Prep Time: 10 min | Cook Time: 0 min

INGREDIENTS:

- 6 cups of fresh baby spinach
- 1/2 cups of split almonds
- 1/2 cup of crumbled goat cheese
- 1/2 cup of dried cranberries
- 1/4 cup of thinly split red onion
- 1/4 cups of balsamic vinaigrette

INSTRUCTIONS:

1. The baby spinach, almonds, goat cheese, cranberries, and red onion should all be mixd in a big salad dish.
2. Pour balsamic vinaigrette over and gently toss to coat.
3. Enjoy your peaceful spinach salad right now.

NUTRITION INFO:

Calories: 180 | Protein: 6g | Carbs: 18g | Fat: 10g | Fiber: 3g | Sugar: 10g

25. RELAXING ROASTED VEGETABLES

Servings: 4 | Prep Time: 10 min | Cook Time: 30 min

INGREDIENTS:

- 1 cups of baby carrots
- 1 cup of broccoli florets
- 1 cup of bell peppers, diced
- 1 cup of zucchini, split
- 2 tbsp olive oil
- 1 tsp dried oregano
- 1 tsp dried basil
- 1/2 tsp garlic powder
- Pepper, & salt as needed

INSTRUCTIONS:

1. Set the oven temp. to 425°F (220°C).
2. Toss the veggies with olive oil, pepper, salt, garlic powder, oregano, and basil in a big bowl.
3. Arrange the veggies on a baking pan so they are in a single layer.
4. Roast the veggies for 25 to 30 min, stirring occasionally, or until they are soft and gently browned.
5. Enjoy your soothing roasted veggies while serving warm.

NUTRITION INFO:

Calories: 160 | Protein: 4g | Carbs: 22g | Fat: 8g | Fiber: 6g | Sugar: 8g

26. BLISSFUL BEETROOT HUMMUS

Servings: 8 | Prep Time: 10 min | Cook Time: 0 min

INGREDIENTS:

- 1 can of washed and drained chickpeas (15 oz.)
- 1 cup of cooked beetroot, peeled and chop-up
- 1/4 cups of tahini
- 2 tbsp lemon juice
- 2 cloves garlic
- 2 tbsp olive oil
- 1/2 tsp ground cumin
- Pepper, & salt as needed
- Fresh parsley for garnish

INSTRUCTIONS:

1. Mix the chickpeas, beetroot, tahini, lemon juice, garlic, olive oil, & cumin in a food processor.
2. Blend until smooth, adding more water as necessary to get the right consistency.
3. As needed, add pepper, & salt for seasoning.
4. Before serving, garnish with fresh parsley. Savor your delicious beetroot hummus as a spread, with pita bread or vegetables.

NUTRITION INFO:

Calories: 120 | Protein: 5g | Carbs: 15g | Fat: 6g | Fiber: 4g | Sugar: 5g

27. GENTLE GINGER AND CARROT SOUP

Servings: 4 | Prep Time: 10 min | Cook Time: 20 min

INGREDIENTS:

- 1 tbsp olive oil
- 1 onion, chop-up
- 2 cloves garlic, chop-up
- 1 tbsp fresh ginger, finely grated
- 4 large carrots, peeled and chop-up
- 4 cups of vegetable broth
- 1/2 cup of coconut milk
- 1/2 tsp ground coriander
- Pepper, & salt as needed

INSTRUCTIONS:

1. Heat the olive oil over medium-heat in a big saucepan, . Sauté the onion and garlic for around five min, or until they are tender.
2. After adding the ginger, simmer for an additional min.
3. After adding the carrots to the vegetable broth, bring it to a boil. Simmer the carrots for fifteen min, or until they are soft, on low heat.
4. Puree the soup by use an immersion blender, or gradually add the soup to a blender until it's smooth.
5. Add the ground coriander and coconut milk and stir. As needed, add pepper, & salt for seasoning.
6. Warm-up and savor your mild carrot and ginger soup.

NUTRITION INFO:

Calories: 180 | Protein: 3g | Carbs: 27g | Fat: 8g | Fiber: 6g | Sugar: 10g

28. ZEN ZESTY LEMON SALMON

Servings: 4 | Prep Time: 10 min | Cook Time: 15 min

INGREDIENTS:

- 4 salmon fillets (about 6 oz every)
- 2 tbsp olive oil
- 2 tbsp lemon juice
- 1 tsp lemon zest
- 2 cloves garlic, chop-up
- 1 tsp dried dill
- Pepper, & salt as needed
- Lemon slices for garnish

INSTRUCTIONS:

1. Set oven temp. to 400°F, or 200°C.
2. Olive oil, lemon juice, lemon zest, garlic, dill, pepper, & salt should all be mixd in a small bowl.
3. Arrange the salmon fillets onto a parchment paper-lined baking sheet. Apply a layer of the lemon mixture.
4. Bake the salmon for 12 to 15 min or until it is cooked through and flakes readily when tested with a fork.
5. Before serving, garnish with slices of lemon. Savor the flavor of your zen lemon salmon.

NUTRITION INFO:

Calories: 280 | Protein: 30g | Carbs: 2g | Fat: 18g | Fiber: 0g | Sugar: 1g

29. MELLOW MANGO SMOOTHIE

Servings: 2 | Prep Time: 5 min | Cook Time: 0 min

INGREDIENTS:

- 1 cup of frozen mango chunks
- 1 banana
- 1 cup of spinach
- 1/2 cup Greek yogurt
- 1 cup of almond milk
- 1 tbsp honey or maple syrup (non-compulsory)

INSTRUCTIONS:

1. Mango chunks, banana, spinach, Greek yogurt, and almond milk should all be mixd in a blender.
2. Process till smooth. To add even more sweetness, feel free to use honey or maple syrup.
3. After pouring into glasses, enjoy your silky mango smoothie.

NUTRITION INFO:

Calories: 230 | Protein: 9g | Carbs: 36g | Fat: 5g | Fiber: 5g | Sugar: 28g

30. PEACEFUL PEVERY PARFAIT

Servings: 4 | Prep Time: 10 min | Cook Time: 0 min

INGREDIENTS:

- 2 cups Greek yogurt
- 1 cup of fresh peveryes, diced (or use canned peveryes, drained)
- 1/2 cup granola
- 1/4 cup honey or maple syrup
- 1/4 cup of chop-up nuts (non-compulsory)
- Fresh mint for garnish (non-compulsory)

INSTRUCTIONS:

1. Arrange the granola, chop-up peveryes, and Greek yogurt in serving dishes or glasses.
2. Drizzle with maple syrup or honey.
3. If desired, sprinkle chop-up nuts on top.
4. Add some mint to the garnish. Serve right away or put in the fridge until you're ready to serve. Savor the tranquil pevery parfait.

NUTRITION INFO:

Calories: 250 | Protein: 12g | Carbs: 35g | Fat: 8g | Fiber: 4g | Sugar: 22g

31. TRANQUIL TOFU STIR-FRY

Servings: 4 | Prep Time: 15 min | Cook Time: 15 min

INGREDIENTS:

- 1 block (14 oz) firm tofu, drained and cubed
- 2 tbsp soy sauce
- 1 tbsp sesame oil
- 1 tbsp hoisin sauce
- 1 cups of bell peppers, split
- 1 cup snap peas
- 1 cup of broccoli florets
- 1 tbsp fresh ginger, chop-up
- 2 cloves garlic, chop-up
- Cooked brown rice or quinoa for serving
- Sesame seeds for garnish (non-compulsory)

INSTRUCTIONS:

1. Sesame oil should be heated in a large wok or pan over medium heat. Add the tofu & simmer for 5-7 min or until golden brown. Take out and place aside from the skillet.
2. Add the garlic & ginger to the same skillet and sauté for 1 min, or until fragrant.
3. Add the broccoli, snap peas, and bell peppers. Stir-fry the veggies for five to seven min, or until they are crisp-tender.
4. Add the hoisin sauce & soy sauce to the pan with the tofu. Toss to coat, then thoroughly cook.
5. Serve over cooked quinoa / brown rice & if preferred, top with sesame seeds. Savor your peaceful stir-fried tofu.

NUTRITION INFO:

Calories: 280 | Protein: 16g | Carbs: 30g | Fat: 14g | Fiber: 6g | Sugar: 8g

32. SOOTHING SAFFRON RICE

Servings: 4 | Prep Time: 5 min | Cook Time: 20 min

INGREDIENTS:

- 1 cup of basmati rice
- 2 cups of vegetable broth
- 1/4 tsp saffron threads
- 1 tbsp olive oil
- 1/2 tsp ground turmeric
- Salt as needed
- Fresh cilantro for garnish (non-compulsory)

INSTRUCTIONS:

1. Till the water runs clear, rinse the basmati rice under cold water.
2. Heat the olive oil in a medium-saucepan over medium heat. After adding the saffron threads and turmeric, simmer for one min.
3. After adding the rice, simmer it for a further min, allowing the spices to coat it.
4. Once added, the vegetable broth should be brought to a boil. Simmer for 15-20 minutes with the lid on and the heat turned down low. The rice should be soft, and the liquid should have been absorbed.
5. Using a fork, fluff and, if wanted, top with fresh cilantro. Enjoy your comforting saffron rice while it's still warm.

NUTRITION INFO:

Calories: 200 | Protein: 4g | Carbs: 40g | Fat: 2g | Fiber: 1g | Sugar: 0g

33. COMFORTING CAULIFLOWER MASH

Servings: 4 | Prep Time: 10 min | Cook Time: 15 min

INGREDIENTS:

- 1 big cauliflower head, cut into small pieces
- 2 tbsp olive oil
- 2 cloves garlic, chop-up
- 1/4 cup finely grated Parmesan cheese
- 1/4 cup of unsweetened almond milk
- Pepper, & salt as needed
- Fresh chives for garnish (non-compulsory)

INSTRUCTIONS:

1. Cauliflower florets should be steamed for ten min or until soft.
2. Blend or mash the potatoes with an immersion mixer in a large bowl until the cauliflower is smooth.
3. Add the almond milk, Parmesan cheese, olive oil, and garlic, and stir. Mix until smooth and thoroughly mixed.
4. As needed, add pepper, & salt for seasoning.
5. If desired, garnish with fresh chives. Warm-up and savor your hearty cauliflower mash.

NUTRITION INFO:

Calories: 120 | Protein: 5g | Carbs: 10g | Fat: 8g | Fiber: 4g | Sugar: 3g

34. CALMING CHIA SEED PUDDING

Servings: 4 | Prep Time: 10 min | Cook Time: 0 min

INGREDIENTS:

- 1/2 cup chia seeds
- 2 cups of almond milk
- 1/4 cup honey or maple syrup
- 1 tsp vanilla extract
- Fresh berries for topping
- Nuts or seeds for garnish (non-compulsory)

INSTRUCTIONS:

1. Chia seeds, almond milk, vanilla essence, and honey or maple syrup should all be mixd in a bowl. Give the chia seeds a good stir to make sure they are spread out evenly.
2. After covering and chilling for a minimum of four hrs or overnight, the chia seeds will absorb the liquid and become thicker.
3. Before serving, give the pudding a stir. If desired, sprinkle some fresh berries, nuts, or seeds over top.
4. Savor the tranquil chia seed pudding.

NUTRITION INFO:

Calories: 180 | Protein: 6g | Carbs: 20g | Fat: 8g | Fiber: 10g | Sugar: 8g

35. BALANCED BROCCOLI SOUP

Servings: 4 | Prep Time: 10 min | Cook Time: 20 min

INGREDIENTS:

- 1 tbsp olive oil
- 1 onion, chop-up
- 2 cloves garlic, chop-up
- 4 cups of broccoli florets
- 2 cups of vegetable broth
- 1/2 cup of unsweetened almond milk
- 1/2 tsp ground nutmeg
- Pepper, & salt as needed

INSTRUCTIONS:

1. Warm up the olive oil in a big saucepan over medium heat. Sauté the onion and garlic for around five min, or until they become tender.
2. Add the veggie broth and broccoli florets. Once the broccoli is cooked, decrease the heat and simmer for 15 min after bringing it to a boil.
3. You can use an immersion blender to make the soup smooth, or you can add the soup to the blender in steps.
4. Add nutmeg and almond milk and stir. As needed, add pepper, & salt for seasoning.
5. Enjoy your well-balanced broccoli soup warm from the pot.

NUTRITION INFO:

Calories: 140 | Protein: 5g | Carbs: 20g | Fat: 6g | Fiber: 6g | Sugar: 5g

36. BLISSFUL BLACK BEAN BURGERS

Servings: 4 | Prep Time: 15 min | Cook Time: 20 min

INGREDIENTS:

- 1 can (15 oz) black beans, cleaned & drained
- 1/2 cup of breadcrumbs
- 1/4 cup lightly chop-up onion
- 1/4 cup lightly chop-up bell pepper
- 1 egg
- 1 tbsp chili powder
- 1 tsp cumin
- 1/2 tsp garlic powder
- Pepper & salt as needed
- Olive oil for cooking

INSTRUCTIONS:

1. In a large bowl, coarsely mash the black beans with a fork / potato masher until they're almost smooth.
2. Add the egg, bell pepper, onion, chili powder, cumin, garlic powder, pepper, & salt, along with the breadcrumbs. Blend until well blended.
3. Create four patties out of the mixture.
4. A little bit of olive oil is added to a pan that is heated over medium heat. Cook the patties until they are crispy and well cooked, 5 to 7 min every side.
5. Top with your preferred toppings and serve on buns. Savor the comfort of your black bean burgers.

NUTRITION INFO:

Calories: 250 | Protein: 12g | Carbs: 30g | Fat: 8g | Fiber: 10g | Sugar: 2g

37. RELAXING RED LENTIL CURRY

Servings: 4 | Prep Time: 10 min | Cook Time: 25 min

INGREDIENTS:

- 1 tbsp olive oil
- 1 onion, chop-up
- 2 cloves garlic, chop-up
- 1 tbsp fresh ginger, chop-up
- 1 cup of red lentils
- 1 can (14.5 oz) diced tomatoes
- 1 can (14 oz) coconut milk
- 1 tbsp curry powder
- 1/2 tsp ground turmeric
- 1/2 tsp ground cumin
- Pepper, & salt as needed
- Fresh cilantro for garnish (non-compulsory)

INSTRUCTIONS:

1. Warm up the olive oil in a big saucepan over medium heat. Add the onion, garlic, & ginger, and cook for approximately 5 min, or until softened.
2. Add the cumin, turmeric, & curry powder, and stir. Cook for one min, or until aromatic.
3. Add the chop-up tomatoes, coconut milk, and red lentils. Bring to a boil when the lentils are cooked, then reduce heat and simmer for 20 min.
4. As needed, add pepper & salt for seasoning.
5. If desired, garnish with fresh cilantro. Warm up and serve with naan or rice. Savor your soothing stew of red lentils.

NUTRITION INFO:

Calories: 280 | Protein: 12g | Carbs: 38g | Fat: 12g | Fiber: 10g | Sugar: 7g

38. HARMONY HERBAL VEGGIE WRAPS

Servings: 4 | Prep Time: 15 min | Cook Time: 0 min

INGREDIENTS:

- 4 large whole wheat tortillas
- 1 cup hummus
- 1 cup of shredded carrots
- 1 cup split cucumber
- 1 cup baby spinach
- 1/2 cup of split bell peppers
- 1/4 cup chop-up fresh herbs (such as parsley, cilantro, or basil)
- Pepper, & salt as needed

INSTRUCTIONS:

1. After arranging the tortillas, top every with a layer of hummus.
2. Evenly distribute the chop-up herbs, bell peppers, cucumber, baby spinach, and shredded carrots over the hummus.
3. As needed, add pepper, & salt for seasoning.
4. Tightly roll the tortillas, cut them in half, and proceed to serve. Savor your vegetarian wraps with herbs and harmony.

NUTRITION INFO:

Calories: 220 | Protein: 8g | Carbs: 35g | Fat: 7g | Fiber: 6g | Sugar: 5g

39. SERENE STRAWBERRY BASIL SALAD

Servings: 4 | Prep Time: 10 min | Cook Time: 0 min

INGREDIENTS:

- 4 cups of mixd greens (such as arugula and spinach)
- 1 cup of fresh strawberries, split
- 1/4 cup of crumbled feta cheese
- 1/4 cup of split almonds
- 1/4 cup fresh basil leaves, torn
- 2 tbsp balsamic vinaigrette

INSTRUCTIONS:

1. The mixed greens, strawberries, feta cheese, almonds, and basil leaves should all be mixd in a big dish.
2. Pour balsamic vinaigrette over and gently toss to coat.
3. Savor your peaceful strawberry basil salad right now.

NUTRITION INFO:

Calories: 180 | Protein: 6g | Carbs: 20g | Fat: 9g | Fiber: 4g | Sugar: 10g

40. MELLOW MINT CHOCOLATE BITES

Servings: 12 | Prep Time: 10 min | Cook Time: 10 min (chilling time)

INGREDIENTS:

- 1 cup of dark chocolate chips
- 1/4 cups of coconut oil
- 1/2 tsp peppermint extract
- 1/4 cup crushed almonds or walnuts (non-compulsory)
- Sea salt for sprinkling (non-compulsory)

INSTRUCTIONS:

1. Melt the coconut oil and dark chocolate chips in a microwave-safe dish, stirring every 30 seconds to ensure a smooth mixture.
2. Add the peppermint essence and stir.
3. Forming tiny clusters, spoon the mixture into silicone molds or onto a baking sheet coated with paper.
4. If preferred, garnish with a sprinkling of sea salt and chop-up walnuts or almonds.
5. To ensure it sets, chill in the fridge for a minimum of one hr. Savor delicious chocolate pieces with a hint of mint.

NUTRITION INFO:

Calories: 120 | Protein: 2g | Fat: 8g | Carbs: 10g | Fiber: 2g | Sugar: 8g

41. QUIET QUINOA BREAKFAST BOWL

Servings: 2 | Prep Time: 10 min | Cook Time: 15 min

INGREDIENTS:

- 1 cup of cooked quinoa
- 1/2 cup of Greek yogurt
- 1/4 cups fresh berries (such as blueberries, raspberries, or strawberries)
- 1 tbsp honey or maple syrup
- 1 tbsp chia seeds
- 1 tbsp nuts / seeds (such as almonds or sunflower seeds)

INSTRUCTIONS:

1. Spoon the cooked quinoa into two separate dishes.
2. Add Greek yogurt, chia seeds, honey or maple syrup, and fresh berries to the top of every bowl.
3. Add a sprinkling of seeds or nuts.
4. For a speedy breakfast, serve straight away or store in the fridge. Savor your peaceful morning dish of quinoa.

NUTRITION INFO:

Calories: 280 | Protein: 12g | Carbs: 40g | Fat: 8g | Fiber: 7g | Sugar: 12g

42. CALM CUCUMBER AND AVOCADO SALAD

Servings: 4 | Prep Time: 10 min | Cook Time: 0 min

INGREDIENTS:

- 2 large cucumbers, split
- 1 large avocado, diced
- 1/4 cup of red onion, thinly split
- 1/4 cup of chop-up fresh dill
- 2 tbsp olive oil
- 1 tbsp lemon juice
- Pepper, & salt as needed

INSTRUCTIONS:

1. Mix the chop-up avocado, red onion, cucumber slices, and dill in a big bowl.
2. Pour in some lemon juice and olive oil.
3. Toss gently to mix, then add pepper, & salt as needed.
4. Enjoy your chilled avocado and cucumber salad right away.

NUTRITION INFO:

Calories: 180 | Protein: 3g | Carbs: 15g | Fat: 13g | Fiber: 7g | Sugar: 4g

43. TRANQUIL TAHINI COOKIES

Servings: 12 | Prep Time: 10 min | Cook Time: 12 min

INGREDIENTS:

- 1/2 cup of tahini
- 1/2 cup of coconut sugar
- 1/4 cup honey or maple syrup
- 1 egg
- 1 tsp vanilla extract
- 1/2 tsp baking soda
- Pinch of salt
- Non-compulsory: 1/4 cup of chocolate chips or chop-up nuts

INSTRUCTIONS:

1. Adjust the oven temp. To 350°F (175°C) and place parchment paper on a baking pan.
2. Mix the tahini, egg, coconut sugar, honey or maple syrup, & vanilla essence in a bowl.
3. Add the salt & baking soda and stir until well mixed.
4. If using, mix in the chocolate chips or almonds.
5. After the baking sheet is ready, drop spoonful's of dough onto it and gently press down to flatten.
6. Bake for ten to twelve min, until the edges are browned.
7. Before moving to a wire rack, let cool for a few minutes on the baking sheet. Savor your peace-loving tahini cookies.

NUTRITION INFO:

Calories: 150 | Protein: 4g | Carbs: 15g | Fat: 9g | Fiber: 2g | Sugar: 8g

44. PEACEFUL PESTO CHICKEN

Servings: 4 | Prep Time: 10 min | Cook Time: 25 min

INGREDIENTS:

- 4 boneless, skinless chicken breasts
- 1/2 cup of basil pesto (store-bought or homemade)
- 1 tbsp olive oil
- Pepper, & salt as needed
- Fresh basil leaves for garnish (non-compulsory)

INSTRUCTIONS:

1. Set the oven temp. to 375°F, or 190°C.
2. Season the chicken breasts with pepper, & salt after rubbing them with olive oil.
3. Evenly coat the chicken breasts with the basil pesto.
4. After putting the chicken in a baking dish, bake it for 20-25 min, or until the internal temp. reveryes 165°F (74°C), indicating that the chicken is done.
5. If desired, garnish with fresh basil leaves. Enjoy your tranquil pesto chicken while it's still warm.

NUTRITION INFO:

Calories: 290 | Protein: 35g | Carbs: 3g | Fat: 15g | Fiber: 1g | Sugar: 2g

45. STRESS-FREE SWEET POTATO FRIES

Servings: 4 | Prep Time: 10 min | Cook Time: 25 min

INGREDIENTS:

- Peel and slice two big sweet potatoes into fries.
- 2 tbsp olive oil
- 1 tsp paprika
- 1/2 tsp garlic powder
- 1/2 tsp onion powder
- Pepper, & salt as needed

INSTRUCTIONS:

1. Adjust the oven temp. To 425°F (220°C) and place parchment paper on a baking pan.
2. The sweet potato fries should be equally coated after being tossed in a big bowl of olive oil, onion powder, paprika, garlic powder, and salt.
3. Arrange the fries on the baking sheet that has been prepared in a single layer.
4. Fries should be baked for 20-25 min, rotating them halfway through, or until they are crispy & golden brown.
5. Enjoy your stress-free sweet potato fries while they're still warm.

NUTRITION INFO:

Calories: 200 | Protein: 2g | Carbs: 30g | Fat: 8g | Fiber: 5g | Sugar: 7g

46. BLISSFUL BLUEBERRY BANANA BREAD

Servings: 8 | Prep Time: 15 min | Cook Time: 60 min

INGREDIENTS:

- 3 ripe bananas, mashed
- 1/2 cup of coconut oil, melted
- 1/2 cup honey or maple syrup
- 2 eggs
- 1 tsp vanilla extract
- 1 1/2 cups whole wheat flour
- 1 tsp baking soda
- 1/2 tsp salt
- 1 cup of fresh or frozen blueberries
- 1/2 tsp ground cinnamon (non-compulsory)

INSTRUCTIONS:

1. Set the oven's temp. to 175°C/350°F. Use oil or parchment paper to line a loaf pan.
2. Mashed bananas, melted coconut oil, eggs, vanilla extract, and honey or maple syrup should all be mixd in a big dish. Blend until well mixd.
3. Mix the flour, baking soda, salt, and cinnamon (if using) in a separate basin.
4. Stirring until just blended, gradually add the dry ingredients to the wet components.
5. Take care not to overmix when you fold in the blueberries.
6. After filling the loaf pan, level the top of the batter.
7. After 50 to 60 minutes in the oven, remove the toothpick from the middle of the loaf; it should come out clean.
8. After letting the bread rest in the pan for ten min, move it to a wire rack to finish cooling. Enjoy your delicious blueberry banana bread by slicing it.

NUTRITION INFO:

Calories: 230 | Protein: 4g | Carbs: 35g | Fat: 9g | Fiber: 3g | Sugar: 18g

47. GENTLE GINGER TEA

Servings: 2 | Prep Time: 5 min | Cook Time: 10 min

INGREDIENTS:

- 2 cups of water
- 1-inch piece of fresh ginger, split
- 1 tbsp honey or maple syrup (non-compulsory)
- 1 tbsp fresh lemon juice (non-compulsory)

INSTRUCTIONS:

1. Heat the water and ginger slices in a small saucepan until they start to boil.
2. For ten min, simmer over low heat.
3. Use a sieve to transfer the tea to individual cups.
4. If preferred, stir in lemon juice and honey or maple syrup.
5. Warm up and enjoy your mild ginger tea.

NUTRITION INFO:

Calories: 20 | Protein: 0g | Carbs: 5g | Fat: 0g | Fiber: 0g | Sugar: 4g

48. HARMONY HERBAL QUINOA

Servings: 4 | Prep Time: 10 min | Cook Time: 15 min

INGREDIENTS:

- 1 cup of quinoa, rinsed
- 2 cups of vegetable broth or water
- 1 tbsp olive oil
- 1 tsp dried thyme
- 1 tsp dried basil
- 1 tsp dried oregano
- 1/2 tsp garlic powder
- Pepper, & salt as needed
- Fresh parsley for garnish (non-compulsory)

INSTRUCTIONS:

1. Quinoa should be mixd with water or vegetable broth in a medium-sized pot. Heat till boiling.
2. After 15 min, or when the quinoa is cooked, and the liquid has been absorbed, reduce heat to low, cover, and simmer.
3. Take the pan from the stove and use a fork to fluff the quinoa.
4. Add the garlic powder, dried thyme, basil, oregano, olive oil, pepper, & salt and stir.
5. If desired, garnish with fresh parsley. Enjoy your harmony herbal quinoa, which is warm and served.

NUTRITION INFO:

Calories: 180 | Protein: 6g | Carbs: 30g | Fat: 5g | Fiber: 3g | Sugar: 1g

49. BALANCED BLACK RICE BOWL

Servings: 4 | Prep Time: 10 min | Cook Time: 30 min

INGREDIENTS:

- 1 cup of black rice, rinsed
- 2 cups of water
- 1 tbsp olive oil
- 1 cups of cooked chickpeas
- 1/2 cups of diced cucumber
- 1/2 cup of shredded carrots
- 1/4 cups of chop-up fresh cilantro
- 2 tbsp tahini
- 1 tbsp lemon juice
- Pepper, & salt as needed

INSTRUCTIONS:

1. Water and black rice should be mixd in a medium pot. Heat till boiling.
2. Simmer, covered, for 30 minutes once rice is soft and water absorbed. Heat on low.
3. Mix the tahini, lemon juice, pepper, & salt in a small bowl.
4. Spoon the cooked rice into every of four bowls.
5. Add fresh cilantro, cucumber, carrots, and chickpeas to the top of every bowl.
6. After serving, drizzle with the tahini dressing. Savor the well-balanced dish of black rice.

NUTRITION INFO:

Calories: 280 | Protein: 8g | Carbs: 45g | Fat: 8g | Fiber: 5g | Sugar: 3g

50. RELAXING RASPBERRY SORBET

Servings: 4 | Prep Time: 5 min | Cook Time: 0 min (+ freezing time)

INGREDIENTS:

- 4 cups of frozen raspberries
- 1/4 cup honey or maple syrup
- 1/4 cups of water
- 1 tbsp lemon juice

INSTRUCTIONS:

1. Put the frozen raspberries, water, lemon juice, honey, or maple syrup in a food processor.
2. Scrape down the sides of the bowl every so often as you blend until smooth.
3. Add a tbsp at a time of more water to the mixture if it's too thick until the right consistency is achieved.
4. Before serving, transfer the sorbet to a freezer-safe container and freeze it for at least two hrs.
5. Enjoy your soothing raspberry sorbet after scooping it.

NUTRITION INFO:

Calories: 100 | Protein: 1g | Carbs: 24g | Fat: 0g | Fiber: 8g | Sugar: 16g

51. ZEN ZUCCHINI FRITTERS

Servings: 4 | Prep Time: 15 min | Cook Time: 15 min

INGREDIENTS:

- 2 large zucchinis, finely grated
- 1/2 tsp salt
- 1/4 cup of flour (whole wheat or almond)
- 1/4 cups of finely grated Parmesan cheese (non-compulsory)
- 1 egg, beaten
- 2 green onions, chop-up
- 1 clove garlic, chop-up
- 1/4 tsp black pepper
- Olive oil for frying

INSTRUCTIONS:

1. To remove moisture, put the shredded zucchini in a strainer, season with salt, and leave for ten min.
2. After squeezing off any extra water, place the zucchini in a basin.
3. Add the egg, green onions, garlic, black pepper, flour, and Parmesan cheese. Blend until well blended.
4. Set a big skillet over medium heat and add a few tbsp of olive oil.
5. Dishfuls of the zucchini mixture should be dropped into the pan and flattened to make fritters.
6. Cook until crispy & golden brown, 3-4 min on every side.
7. Take out of the skillet and pat dry with paper towels. Enjoy your Zen zucchini fritters while they're still warm.

NUTRITION INFO:

Calories: 130 | Protein: 5g | Carbs: 10g | Fat: 8g | Fiber: 2g | Sugar: 2g

52. SERENITY SOUP WITH CHICKPEAS

Servings: 4 | Prep Time: 10 min | Cook Time: 25 min

INGREDIENTS:

- 1 tbsp olive oil
- 1 onion, chop-up
- 2 cloves garlic, chop-up
- 1 carrot, diced
- 1 celery stalk, diced
- 1 tsp ground cumin
- 1 tsp ground coriander
- 1 can of washed and drained chickpeas (15 oz.)
- 4 cups of vegetable broth
- 1/2 cups of quinoa, rinsed
- 2 cups of chop-up spinach
- Pepper, & salt as needed
- Fresh cilantro for garnish (non-compulsory)

INSTRUCTIONS:

1. Warm up the olive oil in a big saucepan over medium heat. Sauté the onion, celery, carrot, and garlic for five min, or until the vegetables are tender.
2. Add the coriander and cumin, and heat for one min, or until fragrant.
3. Add the quinoa, veggie broth, and chickpeas. Once it has reached a boil, lower the heat, & simmer the quinoa for 20 min, or until it is tender and the flavors have mixd.
4. Cook the chop-up spinach for two to three min, or until it wilts.
5. As needed, add pepper, & salt for seasoning. If desired, garnish with fresh cilantro. Enjoy your peaceful soup with chickpeas while it's still warm.

NUTRITION INFO:

Calories: 220 | Protein: 8g | Carbs: 35g | Fat: 5g | Fiber: 8g | Sugar: 4g

53. MELLOW MUSHROOM TACOS

Servings: 4 | Prep Time: 15 min | Cook Time: 15 min

INGREDIENTS:

- 8 small corn tortillas
- 1 tbsp olive oil
- 2 cups of split mushrooms (such as cremini or button)
- 1/2 tsp ground cumin
- 1/2 tsp smoked paprika
- 1/4 tsp garlic powder
- Pepper, & salt as needed
- 1 avocado, split
- 1/2 cup of shredded red cabbage
- 1/4 cups of chop-up fresh cilantro
- Lime wedges for serving

INSTRUCTIONS:

1. A big skillet set over medium heat should be used to warm the olive oil. Add the garlic powder, smoked paprika, cumin, pepper, and salt, along with the cut mushrooms.
2. The mushrooms should be sautéed for 8 to 10 min, or until they become soft and golden.
3. Use a microwave or a dry skillet to reheat the corn tortillas.
4. Spoon the mushrooms onto every tortilla.
5. Add chop-up cilantro, shredded red cabbage, and avocado slices on top.
6. Lime wedges should be served alongside. Savor your tacos with mild mushrooms.

NUTRITION INFO:

Calories: 180 | Protein: 4g | Carbs: 25g | Fat: 8g | Fiber: 6g | Sugar: 2g

54. TRANQUIL TURMERIC RICE

Servings: 4 | Prep Time: 5 min | Cook Time: 20 min

INGREDIENTS:

- 1 cup of basmati rice, rinsed
- 2 cups of water
- 1 tbsp olive oil or ghee
- 1 tsp ground turmeric
- 1/2 tsp ground cumin
- 1/2 tsp salt
- Fresh cilantro for garnish (non-compulsory)

INSTRUCTIONS:

1. Heat ghee/olive oil in a medium saucepan over medium heat. After adding the cumin and turmeric, simmer for one min, or until aromatic.
2. Stir to distribute the spices evenly throughout the washed basmati rice.
3. Add the salt and pour in the water. Next, boil it for a while. lower the heat to a simmer, cover, & let the rice cook for 15 to 20 min, or until it is soft and the water has been absorbed.
4. Using a fork, fluff the rice and, if desired, sprinkle with fresh cilantro. Warm up and enjoy your peaceful turmeric rice.

NUTRITION INFO:

Calories: 180 | Protein: 3g | Carbs: 35g | Fat: 3g | Fiber: 1g | Sugar: 0g

55. CALM CAULIFLOWER AND CHICKPEA CURRY

Servings: 4 | Prep Time: 10 min | Cook Time: 25 min

INGREDIENTS:

- 1 tbsp coconut oil
- 1 onion, chop-up
- 2 cloves garlic, chop-up
- 1-inch piece ginger, chop-up
- 1 tbsp curry powder
- 1/2 tsp ground turmeric
- 1 can (15 oz) coconut milk
- 1 can of washed and drained chickpeas (15 oz.)
- 1 small cauliflower, cut into florets
- 1 cups of vegetable broth
- Pepper, & salt as needed
- Fresh cilantro for garnish (non-compulsory)

INSTRUCTIONS:

1. A large saucepan set over a medium-high heat is ideal for heating coconut oil. Add the onion, garlic, & ginger, and cook for approximately 5 min, or until softened.
2. Add the turmeric and curry powder, and simmer for one min, or until aromatic.
3. Add the cauliflower, chickpeas, and vegetable broth along with the coconut milk. Once the cauliflower is cooked, decrease heat and simmer for 20 min after bringing to a boil.
4. As needed, add pepper, & salt for seasoning. If desired, garnish with fresh cilantro. Enjoy your peaceful curry of cauliflower and chickpeas while it's still warm.

NUTRITION INFO:

Calories: 280 | Protein: 7g | Carbs: 25g | Fat: 18g | Fiber: 7g | Sugar: 5g

56. COMFORTING COCONUT YOGURT PARFAIT

Servings: 4 | Prep Time: 10 min | Cook Time: 0 min

INGREDIENTS:

- 2 cups of coconut yogurt
- 1 cup of granola (gluten-free if needed)
- 1 cups of mixed berries (such as strawberries, blueberries, raspberries)
- 1/4 cups of shredded coconut
- 1 tbsp honey or maple syrup (non-compulsory)

INSTRUCTIONS:

1. Spoon a layer of coconut yogurt onto the bottom of every one of the four serving cups or bowls.
2. Top with granola and then a layer of mixed berries.
3. Once all of the ingredients have been utilized, continue layering them until a layer of berries is on top.
4. If desired, drizzle with honey / maple syrup and top with shredded coconut.
5. Enjoy this cozy coconut yogurt parfait right after serving.

NUTRITION INFO:

Calories: 250 | Protein: 5g | Carbs: 35g | Fat: 10g | Fiber: 5g | Sugar: 15g

57. PEACEFUL PARSLEY PESTO PASTA

Servings: 4 | Prep Time: 10 min | Cook Time: 15 min

INGREDIENTS:

- 12 oz whole wheat or gluten-free pasta
- 2 cups of fresh parsley, packed
- 1/2 cup of walnuts or almonds
- 1/4 cup finely grated Parmesan cheese (non-compulsory)
- 2 cloves garlic
- 1/4 cups of olive oil
- Juice of 1 lemon
- Pepper, & salt as needed
- Cherry tomatoes or grilled vegetables for serving (non-compulsory)

INSTRUCTIONS:

1. When cooking pasta, be sure to follow the package guidelines. After draining, put it away.
2. In a food processor, blend the parsley, garlic, almonds or walnuts, and Parmesan cheese (if desired). Pulse until finely chopped.
3. Add the lemon juice & olive oil gradually while the machine is running and process until smooth. As needed, add pepper, & salt for seasoning.
4. Coat the cooked pasta evenly with the parsley pesto by tossing it.
5. If preferred, serve with grilled veggies or cherry tomatoes. Savor your spaghetti with pesto and parsley in solitude.

NUTRITION INFO:

Calories: 370 | Protein: 10g | Carbs: 45g | Fat: 18g | Fiber: 7g | Sugar: 3g

58. SOOTHING SPINACH AND ARTICHOKE DIP

Servings: 8 | Prep Time: 10 min | Cook Time: 20 min

INGREDIENTS:

- 1 tbsp olive oil
- 1 onion, lightly chop-up
- 2 cloves garlic, chop-up
- 1 package (10 oz) of warmed and drained frozen spinach
- 1 can (14 oz) artichoke hearts, drained and chop-up
- 1/2 cups of Greek yogurt
- 1/2 cup of cream cheese, softened
- 1/2 cup finely grated Parmesan cheese
- 1/2 cup of shredded mozzarella cheese
- Pepper, & salt as needed

INSTRUCTIONS:

1. Set the oven temp. to 375°F, or 190°C.
2. Olive oil should be heated in a big skillet over medium heat. Sauté the onion and garlic for around five min, or until they are tender.
3. Cook for a further three min after adding the spinach and artichokes.
4. Mix the cream cheese, mozzarella, Parmesan, and Greek yogurt together in a mixing basin. Add the artichoke and spinach combination and stir. Add pepper and salt for seasoning.
5. When the mixture is bubbling and brown on top, bake it in a baking dish for 15 to 20 min.
6. Warm spinach and artichoke dip should be served with whole-grain crackers or vegetable sticks for a calming treat.

NUTRITION INFO:

Calories: 150 | Protein: 6g | Carbs: 6g | Fat: 11g | Fiber: 2g | Sugar: 2g

59. BALANCED BUCKWHEAT PANCAKES

Servings: 4 | Prep Time: 10 min | Cook Time: 15 min

INGREDIENTS:

- 1 cup of buckwheat flour
- 1/2 cups of almond flour
- 1 tsp baking powder
- 1/2 tsp baking soda
- 1/4 tsp salt
- 1 tbsp honey or maple syrup
- 1 cup almond milk / other plant-based milk
- 1 large egg
- 1 tbsp melted coconut oil or butter
- 1 tsp vanilla extract
- Fresh berries or split bananas for serving (non-compulsory)

INSTRUCTIONS:

1. Mix the buckwheat flour, almond flour, baking soda, baking powder, and salt in a big basin.
2. Mix the egg, melted coconut oil, almond milk, honey or maple syrup, & vanilla extract in a separate dish.
3. Mixing until just mixed, pour the wet components into the dry ingredients.
4. Over medium heat, preheat a nonstick skillet or griddle. Apply butter or coconut oil sparingly.
5. For every pancake, add 1/4 cup of batter to the skillet. Cook for a further two to three min after flipping or until bubbles appear on the surface.
6. Savor your well-proportioned buckwheat pancakes warm, accompanied with split bananas or fresh berries.

NUTRITION INFO:

Calories: 220 | Protein: 6g | Carbs: 28g | Fat: 10g | Fiber: 5g | Sugar: 4g

60. BLISSFUL BANANA OAT BARS

Servings: 12 | Prep Time: 10 min | Cook Time: 25 min

INGREDIENTS:

- 2 ripe bananas, mashed
- 1/4 cup honey / maple syrup
- 1/4 cups of almond butter
- 1 tsp vanilla extract
- 2 cups of rolled oats
- 1/2 tsp ground cinnamon
- 1/4 cup of dark chocolate chips (non-compulsory)
- 1/4 cup of chop-up nuts (non-compulsory)

INSTRUCTIONS:

1. Set the oven's temp. to 175°C/350°F. Using parchment paper, line an 8 × 8-inch baking sheet.
2. The mashed bananas, almond butter, honey or maple syrup, and vanilla extract should all be mixd in a big bowl. Blend until well mixd.
3. Add the ground cinnamon, rolled oats, and non-compulsory chocolate chips and nuts and stir.
4. Fill the baking pan with the mixture and press it down firmly.
5. Bake for twenty to twenty-five min, or until the sides are browned.
6. Let cool completely before slicing into bars. Savor your delightful bars of banana oats.

NUTRITION INFO:

Calories: 160 | Protein: 3g | Carbs: 25g | Fat: 6g | Fiber: 3g | Sugar: 9g

61. RELAXING ROASTED RED PEPPER HUMMUS

Servings: 8 | Prep Time: 10 min | Cook Time: 0 min

INGREDIENTS:

- 1 can of washed and drained chickpeas (15 oz.)
- 1 large roasted red pepper, chop-up
- 2 tbsp tahini
- 2 tbsp olive oil
- 1 clove garlic, chop-up
- Juice of 1 lemon
- 1/2 tsp ground cumin
- Pepper, & salt as needed
- Paprika and fresh parsley for garnish (non-compulsory)

INSTRUCTIONS:

1. The chickpeas, tahini, garlic, lemon juice, cumin, and roasted red pepper should all be mixd in a food processor. Process till smooth.
2. As needed, add pepper, & salt for seasoning. Add a little water or more lemon juice to thin down the hummus if it's too thick.
3. If preferred, top with fresh parsley and paprika after transferring to a serving dish.
4. Savor this soothing roasted red pepper hummus with crackers, pita bread, or fresh veggies.

NUTRITION INFO:

Calories: 100 | Protein: 3g | Carbs: 10g | Fat: 5g | Fiber: 3g | Sugar: 1g

62. GENTLE GREEN PEA SOUP

Servings: 4 | Prep Time: 10 min | Cook Time: 20 min

INGREDIENTS:

- 1 tbsp olive oil
- 1 onion, chop-up
- 2 cloves garlic, chop-up
- 4 cups of green peas (fresh or frozen)
- 4 cups of vegetable broth
- 1/2 tsp dried thyme
- 1/2 tsp salt
- 1/4 tsp black pepper
- 1/4 cups of fresh mint leaves (non-compulsory)
- 1/4 cups of coconut milk (non-compulsory)

INSTRUCTIONS:

1. Warm up the olive oil in a big saucepan over medium heat. Sauté the onion and garlic for around five min, or until they are tender.
2. Stir in the thyme, vegetable broth, green peas, pepper, & salt. Simmer the peas for 10–15 min, or until they reach a mushy consistency, after the water boils.
3. Toss in the coconut milk and, if using, the fresh mint leaves. Then, purée the soup until it's completely smooth using an immersion blender. Alternately, put in batches to a blender and process until smooth.
4. Enjoy your mild green pea soup fresh from the stove.

NUTRITION INFO:

Calories: 180 | Protein: 7g | Carbs: 30g | Fat: 5g | Fiber: 8g | Sugar: 9g

63. TRANQUIL THAI CURRY

Servings: 4 | Prep Time: 15 min | Cook Time: 25 min

INGREDIENTS:

- 1 tbsp coconut oil
- 1 onion, split
- 2 cloves garlic, chop-up
- 1 tbsp red curry paste
- 1 can (14 oz) coconut milk
- 1 cups of vegetable broth
- 1 red bell pepper, split
- 1 zucchini, split
- 1 cups of baby spinach
- 1 cup of firm tofu, cubed (non-compulsory)
- 2 tbsp soy sauce or tamari
- 1 tbsp lime juice
- Fresh basil or cilantro for garnish

INSTRUCTIONS:

1. A large saucepan set over medium heat is ideal for heating coconut oil. Sauté the onion and garlic for around five min, or until they are tender.
2. Add the red curry paste & stir until aromatic, about 1 min.
3. Stir together the vegetable broth & coconut milk after adding them. Heat through to a simmer.
4. Add the zucchini, red bell pepper, and, if using, tofu. Simmer the veggies for ten to fifteen min, or until they are soft.
5. Add the lime juice, soy sauce, and baby spinach and stir. Cook the spinach for a further two to three min, or until it wilts.
6. Relax with your Thai curry after serving it warm and adding some fresh cilantro or basil as a garnish.

NUTRITION INFO:

Calories: 260 | Protein: 8g | Carbs: 20g | Fat: 18g | Fiber: 4g | Sugar: 6g

64. SERENE SWEET POTATO AND BLACK BEAN CHILI

Servings: 4 | Prep Time: 10 min | Cook Time: 30 min

INGREDIENTS:

- 1 tbsp olive oil
- 1 onion, chop-up
- 2 cloves garlic, chop-up
- 1 large sweet potato, peeled and diced
- 1 red bell pepper, chop-up
- Black beans, 15 ounces (can), washed and drained
- 1 can (14 oz) diced tomatoes
- 1 cups of vegetable broth
- 1 tsp ground cumin
- 1 tsp chili powder
- 1/2 tsp smoked paprika
- Pepper, & salt as needed
- Fresh cilantro for garnish (non-compulsory)

INSTRUCTIONS:

1. Warm up the olive oil in a big saucepan over medium heat. Sauté the onion and garlic for around five min, or until they are tender.
2. Cook for a further five min after adding the chop-up red bell pepper and sweet potato.
3. Add the cumin, chili powder, smoked paprika, chop-up tomatoes, black beans, vegetable broth, pepper, & salt.
4. After it boils, reduce the heat & cook the sweet potato for around 20 to 25 min, or until it becomes tender.
5. Savor your peaceful sweet potato and black bean chili while it's still warm, and if you'd like, top with fresh cilantro.

NUTRITION INFO:

Calories: 220 | Protein: 7g | Carbs: 40g | Fat: 5g | Fiber: 10g | Sugar: 9g

65. CALM CARROT AND GINGER SMOOTHIE

Servings: 2 | Prep Time: 5 min | Cook Time: 0 min

INGREDIENTS:

- 2 large carrots, peeled and chop-up
- 1-inch piece fresh ginger, peeled & finely grated
- 1 banana, split
- 1/2 cups of orange juice
- 1/2 cups almond milk / other plant-based milk
- 1 tbsp honey or maple syrup (non-compulsory)
- Ice cubes (non-compulsory)

INSTRUCTIONS:

1. Finely grated ginger, banana, orange juice, almond milk, split carrots, and honey or maple syrup, if used, should all be mixd in a blender.
2. If you want a more excellent smoothie, add ice cubes and blend until smooth.
3. Pour into glasses and enjoy your peaceful smoothie made with carrots and ginger.

NUTRITION INFO:

Calories: 150 | Protein: 2g | Carbs: 35g | Fat: 1g | Fiber: 5g | Sugar: 25g

66. PEACEFUL POMEGRANATE SALAD

Servings: 4 | Prep Time: 10 min | Cook Time: 0 min

INGREDIENTS:

- 4 cups of mixd greens (such as arugula, spinach, and kale)
- 1/2 cups of pomegranate seeds
- 1/4 cup of walnuts, chop-up
- 1/4 cup of feta cheese, crumbled (non-compulsory)
- 1 avocado, split
- 2 tbsp olive oil
- 1 tbsp balsamic vinegar
- 1 tsp honey or maple syrup
- Pepper, & salt as needed

INSTRUCTIONS:

1. If used, avocado slices, walnuts, pomegranate seeds, and feta cheese should all be mixd in a big salad dish.
2. To create the dressing, mix the olive oil, balsamic vinegar, honey (or maple syrup), pepper, & salt in a small bowl.
3. Over the salad, drizzle with the dressing and toss lightly to mix.
4. Quickly serve and enjoy your serene pomegranate salad.

NUTRITION INFO:

Calories: 200 | Protein: 4g | Carbs: 14g | Fat: 16g | Fiber: 6g | Sugar: 8g

67. HARMONY HERBAL GREEN JUICE

Servings: 2 | Prep Time: 10 min | Cook Time: 0 min

INGREDIENTS:

- 2 cups of kale or spinach
- 1 cucumber, peeled and chop-up
- 2 celery stalks, chop-up
- 1 green apple, chop-up
- 1-inch piece fresh ginger, peeled
- 1/2 lemon, juiced
- 1 cup of cold water or coconut water

INSTRUCTIONS:

1. The kale or spinach, cucumber, celery, green apple, ginger, lemon juice, and either cold water or coconut water should all be mixd in a blender.
2. If you want a smoother texture, strain the juice through a cheesecloth / a fine mesh screen after blending until it's smooth.
3. Enjoy your herbal green juice in peace after pouring it into glasses.

NUTRITION INFO:

Calories: 80 | Protein: 2g | Carbs: 20g | Fat: 0g | Fiber: 5g | Sugar: 12g

68. STRESS-FREE SHRIMP STIR-FRY

Servings: 4 | Prep Time: 10 min | Cook Time: 15 min

INGREDIENTS:

- 1 tbsp sesame oil
- 1-lb shrimp, peeled and deveined
- 1 red bell pepper, split
- 1 yellow bell pepper, split
- 1 zucchini, split
- 2 cloves garlic, chop-up
- 1 tbsp soy sauce or tamari
- 1 tbsp honey or maple syrup
- 1 tbsp rice vinegar
- 1 tsp finely grated fresh ginger
- Cooked brown rice or quinoa for serving

INSTRUCTIONS:

1. Turn up the heat to medium-high in a big wok or pan and add the sesame oil.
2. Sauté the shrimp for two to three min, or until they are opaque and pink. Take out and place aside from the skillet.
3. Add the garlic, zucchini, and bell peppers to the same skillet. Stir-fry the veggies for five to seven min, or until they become soft.
4. Mix the rice vinegar, finely grated ginger, honey, tamari or soy sauce, and maple syrup in a small bowl.
5. Cover the stir-fry with the sauce after adding the shrimp back to the pan. Stir to coat everything in the sauce, and cook for another two minutes.
6. Enjoy your stress-free dinner after serving the shrimp stir-fry over cooked brown rice or quinoa.

NUTRITION INFO:

Calories: 240 | Protein: 25g | Carbs: 20g | Fat: 7g | Fiber: 3g | Sugar: 9g

69. BLISSFUL BEET AND BERRY SMOOTHIE

Servings: 2 | Prep Time: 5 min | Cook Time: 0 min

INGREDIENTS:

- 1 small beet, cooked and chop-up
- 1/2 cups of mixed berries (such as strawberries, blueberries, and raspberries)
- 1 banana, split
- 1 cups almond milk / other plant-based milk
- 1 tbsp chia seeds
- 1 tsp honey or maple syrup (non-compulsory)

INSTRUCTIONS:

1. Blend together the cooked beet, banana, almond milk, chia seeds, mixed berries, and honey or maple syrup, if desired, in a blender.
2. Add more almond milk if necessary and blend until smooth to get the right consistency.
3. Pour into glasses, then enjoy your delicious smoothie with berries and beets.

NUTRITION INFO:

Calories: 140 | Protein: 3g | Carbs: 30g | Fat: 3g | Fiber: 7g | Sugar: 18g

70. SOOTHING SESAME NOODLES

Servings: 4 | Prep Time: 10 min | Cook Time: 10 min

INGREDIENTS:

- 8 oz whole wheat or rice noodles
- 2 tbsp sesame oil
- 2 tbsp soy sauce or tamari
- 1 tbsp rice vinegar
- 1 tbsp honey or maple syrup
- 1 clove garlic, chop-up
- 1 tsp finely grated fresh ginger
- 1 tbsp tahini or peanut butter
- 1/2 tsp red pepper flakes (non-compulsory)
- 2 green onions, split
- 1/4 cups of chop-up cilantro
- 1 tbsp sesame seeds

INSTRUCTIONS:

1. The package will tell you how to boil the noodles. To cease cooking, drain and rinse with cold water.
2. Mix the sesame oil, rice vinegar, honey, maple syrup, tahini or peanut butter, ginger, garlic, and red pepper flakes (if using) in a big bowl.
3. Coat the noodles well by tossing them in the sauce.
4. Add sesame seeds, cilantro, and green onions as garnish.
5. Savor your comforting sesame noodles at room temp. Or cold.

NUTRITION INFO:

Calories: 280 | Protein: 7g | Carbs: 45g | Fat: 10g | Fiber: 4g | Sugar: 5g

71. ZEN ZESTY LIME AVOCADO SALAD

Servings: 4 | Prep Time: 10 min | Cook Time: 0 min

INGREDIENTS:

- 2 ripe avocados, diced
- 1 cup of cherry tomatoes, halved
- 1/2 red onion, thinly split
- 1/4 cup of fresh cilantro, chop-up
- 1/4 cups fresh lime juice (about 2 limes)
- 2 tbsp olive oil
- Pepper, & salt as needed
- 1/4 tsp ground cumin
- 1/4 tsp chili powder (non-compulsory)

INSTRUCTIONS:

1. Mix the chop-up avocados, cherry tomatoes, red onion, and cilantro in a large salad dish.
2. Mix the lime juice, olive oil, cumin, salt, pepper, and chili powder (if using) in a small bowl.
3. Toss the salad lightly to combine after dressing it.
4. Enjoy your zen-inspired, zesty lime avocado salad right away after serving.

NUTRITION INFO:

Calories: 220 | Protein: 2g | Carbs: 12g | Fat: 20g | Fiber: 8g | Sugar: 2g

72. TRANQUIL TURMERIC TEA

Servings: 2 | Prep Time: 5 min | Cook Time: 5 min

INGREDIENTS:

- 2 cup ofs almond milk or other plant-based milk
- 1 tsp ground turmeric
- 1/2 tsp ground cinnamon
- 1/4 tsp ground ginger
- 1 tbsp honey or maple syrup
- 1/2 tsp vanilla extract
- Pinch of black pepper

INSTRUCTIONS:

1. Almond milk, black pepper, vanilla essence, turmeric, ginger, cinnamon, and maple syrup should all be mixd in a small pot.
2. Cook, whisking continuously, over medium-low heat until heated but not boiling.
3. Transfer into cups and enjoy your soothing turmeric tea.

NUTRITION INFO:

Calories: 100 | Protein: 1g | Carbs: 18g | Fat: 3g | Fiber: 2g | Sugar: 15g

73. CALM CARAMELIZED ONION AND GOAT CHEESE TART

Servings: 6 | Prep Time: 20 min | Cook Time: 40 min

INGREDIENTS:

- 1 pre-made pie crust (or homemade)
- 3 large onions, thinly split
- 2 tbsp olive oil
- 1 tbsp balsamic vinegar
- 1 tsp fresh thyme leaves / half a tsp dried thyme
- 4 oz goat cheese, crumbled
- 1/4 cup finely grated Parmesan cheese
- Pepper & salt as needed

INSTRUCTIONS:

1. Set the oven temp. to 375°F, or 190°C. Roll out your pie crust and line a tart pan with it. Cut off any extra dough.
2. Olive oil should be heated in a big skillet over medium heat. Add the split onions and simmer for approximately 25 to 30 min, stirring now and again, until they are caramelized and golden brown.
3. Add the thyme, salt, pepper, and balsamic vinegar and stir. After cooking for two more min, turn off the heat.
4. Evenly distribute the caramelized onions across the pie shell. Top with finely grated Parmesan cheese and goat cheese crumbles.
5. In a preheated oven, bake for 15-20 min, or until the cheese is melted and the crust is brown

6. Let it cool somewhat before slicing and serving. Savor your peaceful tart with goat cheese and caramelized onions.

NUTRITION INFO:

Calories: 280 | Protein: 7g | Carbs: 24g | Fat: 18g | Fiber: 2g | Sugar: 6g

74. SERENE SPINACH AND FETA STUFFED CHICKEN

Servings: 4 | Prep Time: 15 min | Cook Time: 30 min

INGREDIENTS:

- 4 boneless, skinless chicken breasts
- 1 cup of fresh spinach, chop-up
- 1/2 cup of crumbled feta cheese
- 2 cloves garlic, chop-up
- 1 tbsp olive oil
- 1 tsp dried oregano
- Pepper, & salt as needed
- 1 tbsp lemon juice

INSTRUCTIONS:

1. Set the oven temp. to 375°F, or 190°C.
2. Add the chop-up garlic, crumbled feta cheese, chop-up spinach, olive oil, oregano, pepper, & salt to a small bowl.
3. Make sure not to cut all the way through when slicing a pocket into every chicken breast. Pack the spinach and feta mixture into every pocket.
4. If needed, fasten the chicken breasts with toothpicks before putting them in a baking dish.
5. Pour in a little more olive oil and lemon juice. Bake for 25-30 min in a preheated oven or until the chicken is well-cooked and its juices are clear.
6. When serving, take out the toothpicks and savor your peaceful chicken packed with spinach and feta.

NUTRITION INFO:

Calories: 250 | Protein: 30g | Carbs: 2g | Fat: 13g | Fiber: 1g | Sugar: 1g

75. BALANCED BANANA AND ALMOND SMOOTHIE

Servings: 2 | Prep Time: 5 min | Cook Time: 0 min

INGREDIENTS:

- 2 ripe bananas, split
- 1/4 cup of almond butter
- 1 cup ofs almond milk or other plant-based milk
- 1 tbsp chia seeds
- 1/2 tsp ground cinnamon
- 1 tsp honey or maple syrup (non-compulsory)
- Ice cubes (non-compulsory)

INSTRUCTIONS:

1. Split bananas, almond butter, almond milk, chia seeds, ground cinnamon, and honey or maple syrup, if desired, should all be mixd in a blender.
2. If you want a more excellent smoothie, add ice cubes and blend until smooth.
3. Enjoy your well-balanced banana and almond smoothie after pouring it into glasses.

NUTRITION INFO:

Calories: 220 | Protein: 5g | Carbs: 32g | Fat: 10g | Fiber: 5g | Sugar: 18g

Printed in Great Britain
by Amazon

49882726R00051